From Within My Heart

Lashonda Binns

Presentation by *BookLeaf Publishing*

Web: www.bookleafpub.com

E-mail: info@bookleafpub.com

ISBN: 9789357744928

First edition 2023

I dedicate From Within My Heart to the loving memory of my uncles, Lloyd Collins, Robert Binns, and Leroy (Debo) Davis; family friend, Mr. James Green, the Best Barber of Southeast Arkansas; my cousin, Karen Binns; and my friend, Aletha McArthur.

ACKNOWLEDGEMENT

I would like to thank my Bestie, Mr. Andre Dobbs, who stood by my side listening and encouraging me to publish and share my writing. Thank you to my family (Bessie and Johnnie Jefferson, Dewey Binns, Retha and Lloyd Collins, Ramona Collins, Dewey Binns II and Amber Bailey-Winn, and Roderick Binns) who always support me in following my dreams. Thank you to my advanced placement English teachers (Mrs. Burton and Mrs. Fakouri) of Monticello High School and my Creative Writing and English teachers at Mississippi Delta Community College. Thank you to the loves lost and gained throughout my years. Most of all I thank God for blessing me with the words and ability to write. Thank you Bookleaf Publishing Team for your support and giving me the opportunity to become a published author.

PREFACE

From Within My Heart is a compilation of poems that I have written over the years. I developed a love for writing in my youth. I always liked to write about my feelings and things I saw going on around me. I learned to write prayers to see when God answers. I found writing was cleansing to the soul. I even made up rhymes to teach youth.

This is an inspiring work of poetry that takes you through the emotions and thoughts of a child, teenager, young adult, parent, lover, friend, daughter, and christian finding their way through life's ups and downs.

You Say You Love Me

You always say that you love me.
 If you love me, why must you always lie?
 If it is love that you have for me, why do you
always make me cry?
 You always say, "I want to see you."
 When the time comes to be face to face, you're
never around.
 It's just a disgrace.
 I've never loved the way I love you.
 But now it's time to tell you that we are through.
 There is no longer us.
 It's me and there's you.
 All because your love for me is Not True!!!!!

The Race

I'm running this race.
Sometimes I fall into last place.
I grow tired as the others fall out of my sight.
Just when I say I'm ready to quit.
I see a light.
I burst into a lightening sprint.
I'm gaining on my opponents!
What a sight?
How marvelous is it to see the light?
One by one I've overcome.
At last, my race is won!

I Am A Fatherless Child

I am a fatherless child.
 Don't get me wrong.
 My Father has just gone wild.
 He says he loves me, but he is a man I never see.
 Once in a while, I talk to him over the phone.
 However, when Momma and me are in his town.
 How convenient it is that he's never around?
 I am a Fatherless child.
 Not because he's dead or even considered a deadbeat Dad.
 I am a Fatherless child because this man is sad, tired, and unavailable.
 He doesn't know me.
 So, why should I continue to seek him?
 I ask to see him and my mom takes us up the road.
 However, I may as well ask to see the prince that was a toad.
 He doesn't have time for me.
 Now this I see.
 I fall into the category of no mommy, no me.
 This is why I am a Fatherless child.

Love's Cost

Take the time to listen to my hurting heartbeat.
 Listen to the pounding of my heart and my
running feet.
 Can you chase the tears that have fallen from
my eyes?
 My heart's longing for your love slowly dies.
 Now my weeping eyes' wells are dry.
 So use to being hurt that I can no longer cry.
 Nor remain in love's race.
 My heart has no more grace.
 Reddened eyes that never lie.
 No longer can I give an alibi.
 All the gloves are off.
 My heart's thirst for you caused me to choke.
 No more words I spoke.
 I can't 'til I cough.
 My love has lost.
 Yet I'm the one who paid the cost.

Don't Cry Anymore

Don't cry anymore.
God has a new blessing in store.
Just do his will.
You will receive a great new thrill.
That old flame didn't last.
Let it be a lesson and place it in the past.
God's light is shining down on you.
Feel his love, for it is always true.
Depend on God.
Lean on His solid staff and rod.
Weeping may endure during the night.
But your joy is coming with the morning light.

Pray

When life presents a stumbling block.
Fall down on your knees to pray.
Man is not the answer at the end of a day.
Man is only a sidekick with whom you explore.
God is a Father. brother, mother, sister, lover,
friend, and so much more!
When you learn to depend on God.
You'll learn there is so much more, in life, to
live for.
Don't run from the road you faced before.
Just understand that it took God to walk away
and close that lonely, painful door.
It is always the Latter Rain that erases the pain
and leads you to what God has in store.
When you face doubt and adversity,
Fall down on your knees to pray.
Let God Lead the way.

Believe

Sometimes life can get you down.
 There comes a point when you no longer hear
the sounds.
 Everything seems so vague.
 It's like an outer body experience that refuses to
end.
 In the midst of the experience, one receives a
sonic boom!
 It's a wake up call to return to reality.
 When life gets you down; just keep going,
going, going...
 In the end the extra drive and determination will
pay off.
 Never give up on your dreams.
 Hard work and extra effort combined with
determination and will power only helps boost
your confidence.
 Even when others don't believe in you.
 If you keep the faith and try really hard, in the
end, you can do all things through Christ who
strengthens you.
 Just Believe!
 And You Can Achieve!

My Friend

A dearer friend no one has ever known.
God always places us with one of his own.
In times of need or in times of sorrow, we
always know who holds tomorrow.
It was not a matter of chance that you and I ever
met.
It was all in God's plan.
Because a true friend was in demand.
It is a friendship that we will never regret.
For that matter no one will ever forget.
A true friend like you is hard to find.
To make it short, you are one of a kind!
Keep smiling and praying, but most of all, never
stop being the beautiful friend I know and love.
You have always been a joy in my heart.
I keep you close in my mind, heart, thoughts,
and prayer even when it seems that I am not
there.
So stay sweet and be strong.
Most of all remember even when we are apart
you are never alone!!

On My Father's Shoulders

On my Father's shoulders did I lye and cry.
On my Father's shoulders did I sit and ride.
On my Father's shoulders did he not put me to
sleep.
On my Father's shoulders did I not learn to pray.
On my Father's shoulders did a head not rest
full of wisdom.
On my Father's shoulders did not the face of
love and kindness show.
On my Father's shoulders did the mouth full of
words of knowledge not rest.
On my Father's shoulders did God place the
hands of a potter to mold me as his piece of clay.
Through the years of my life, God used my
Father's shoulders as a guide to be the center that
never changed.
No matter what had to be rearranged in my life,
it was always upon my Father's shoulders that a
little girl like me could always rely.

Why Must Our Children Go Astray

Why must our children go astray?
Did you not hear me when I prayed?
Was it something I said?
Or something I might have thought or done?
Was it a stone I cast when out done?
Was it a flash from my tongue?
Maybe a spiritual battle not won.
Lord, was it my yelling and cursing time and time again.
Never learning how to reach out while listening deep within.
I missed the sound of my child's tender cry.
I forgot how to sing the loving words of the lullaby.
I didn't try to feel the presence of our warm embrace.
I was to busy running my own private race.
Yes, I forgot how to make time, just for us.
No longer am I the one my child trusts.
It's the love my child found in a gang.
Or in the teenage love that brought on so much pain!
The high of drugs bought off the block.
Or maybe the rush of cocking a glock.

I didn't see what lay ahead
20 to life in a cell living among the dead.
Then taking my child straight to hell on a death
bed.
All because I forgot how to exhale.

Down On My Knees

Down on my knees I pray.
Dear Lord, help me through this day.
Keep me near thee so I may not stray.
So many debts I must pay.
Train my mind and heart to be filled with you,
your ways, and your love.
Lord, reach down from above.
Rock me in the cradle of your arms.
As I tread through life's storms.
Dark is the way, but your light brightens my
path.
Please shield me from all wrath.
Open my ears to hear.
Let me not walk in fear.
Cleanse my weeping eyes from the pain filled
tears.
Heal thine aching and wounded heart.
Today I make a new start.
Lord, I am seeking your will in my life.
I am not defeated by misery or strife.
I call unto thee seeking your counsel.
Let your wisdom overflow from my lips as my
life excels.
Guide me in all that I do to avoid life's evil
spells.

Order my steps Lord, down on my knees I shall
forever pray.
Each and every day.
No matter come what may.
Down on my knees I shall forever pray.

When Life Passes You By

When life passes you by,
 do you sit around and cry?
When life passes you by,
 do you ever take a stand?
When life passes you by,
 do you ever take chances?
When life passes you by,
 do you try new things?
When life passes you by,
 do you live by a routine?
When life passes you by,
 do you ever express how you feel?
When life passes you by,
 do you think you were wronged?
When life passes you by,
 do you say this is why I act this way?
When life passes you by,
 do you believe this is all you deserve?
When life passes you by,
 do you ever think I'm tired?
When life passes you by,
 do you ever finally say, "Jesus help me, I am
gonna change today?"

Can You Love Me

15

Can you love me for life?
Can you love me and make me your wife?
Can you love me through the misery?
Can you love me in strife?
Can you love me enough to hold me?
Can you love me enough to touch me?
Can you love me with your smile?
Can you love me with your kiss?
Can you love me in the sunshine and rain?
Can you love me until the end of time?
The true question is not can you love me, but
will you love me?

Breakthrough

God trouble is all around me.
Friends' hands have proven untrue.
Flipping on me and trying me too.
Don't take me there.
I will lose my cool; dance with them too!
I'm running to you, God.
Feed me cause I need your staff and rod.
I don't want to be like Peter.
I am loving by choice, but a fighter with a one
hitter quiter.
A tongue that cuts through the source.
Lord keep my course.
God you Saved me from the snare.
They looked at me with a stare.
They were talking about me and even said it to
my face.
I was looking and responded with words that
were a disgrace.
Oh, now they look amazed and shocked.
Cause they mind was rocked.
I clicked and punched that clock.
Funny thing about it.
Others gave me clout.
God had to work it out.
Cause my soul was disturbed.

My heart and mind perturbed.
I had no empathy and was out of my element.
Feeling the descent.
I fell from grace.
Stumbled in my race.
Realizing I was betrayed and frayed.
I reacted and was not proactive.
God had given my sword and shield.
He even gave me words to speak, "Peace be still."
God even showed me when Jesus calmed the raging sea.
This is how I need to be.
Eased in my mind, soul, and spirit.
Truly free to be uniquely fit.
Never allowing the enemy to spit.
God gave me more wit.
I got my breakthrough.
I am free with my que.
God taught me the signs.
Now I create my own designs.
Control my own tunes.
Singing with the croons.
Thank you, Lord, for my breakthrough!

How Sweet it is

Sugared down.
 White or brown.
 Coarse and fine.
 Original or made by design.
 Natural or man-made.
 Outside or in the shade.
 Desire for you remains the same.
 How sweet it is?
 In cakes or ice creams.
 As we are awake or in dreams.
 Tasting you in dessert or fine cuisine.
 Used in facial scrubs or body rubs feeling
serene.
 Blasted like sand.
 Rubbed within my hands.
 A mouth full of heaven.
 How sweet it is?
 Your body dances and your voice sings.
 Your mouth twists and your tongue rings.
 Oh the joy from within.
 Squeezing your cheeks, here's a grin.
 Your mind signals, oh more!
 Solids, liquids, whatever is in store.
 Your taste buds implore, "Mi Amor!"
 How sweet it is?

Oh Music

Sound waves flowing like the wind in a smooth,
calming summer breeze.
 A crescendo equal to a sudden sneeze.
 Oh Music!
 The vibrato flutters like humming bird's wings.
 Allegro brings cheer like a kid with new things.
 Legato is smooth and connected like the Golden
State Warriors at their peak.
 Each tune is subliminally unique with each
tweak.
 Oh Music!
 Melody sets the trend.
 While Harmony stacks the notes to blend.
 From the Cadence with it's punctuation like the
platoon doing their march.
 To the Chromatic notes which have a dip and
arch.
 Oh Music!
 The Overture introduction.
 Leading to the Obbligato which is the key to the
composition.
 The Sonata serenade,
 As the Chorus begins it's escapade.

Out come Soprano, Alto, Tenor, Baritone, and
Bass.
Oh Music!
You travel so many places.
While you expose your many faces.
Oh Music!
I see Jazz, Dance, Latin, R & B, Techno,
Gospel, Opera, Classical, and even Rap Hip Hop
with Country Western.
I can't forget Rock, Pop, or kids Bop, or
Contemporary Christian.
Oh Music!
You are just right for me.

Keep Running From These Streets

Keep running from these streets!
Mysterious and alluring are they to be engaged.
All the unknowns that parents dissuade.
Keep running from these streets!
The urban male who has finesse.
Even the sly fox whose tongue and dress puts
any female in distress.
Keep running from these streets!
The beauty queens who can't dodge the sheets.
Street runners who slay that beat.
Keep running from these streets!
Every reason you stay home to play.
Avoid the nightlife and survive in the day.
Keep running from these streets!
Many say talk is cheap.
That is until you're in to deep.
Keep running from these streets!
Every thing began as a fun game.
Until every move became a walk of shame.
Keep running from these streets!
You were the hottest thing we ever seen.
Then you fell and you lost your sheen.
Keep running from these streets!
Wishing you heard the word and stayed away.

Now everything and everyone has gone astray.
Now you wish you kept running from these
streets.

I'm Moving On

Here I stand.
Holding the key in my hand.
Where do I go from here?
I'm moving on.
I am down on my luck.
Time is passing me by cause I am stuck.
Where do I go from here?
I'm moving on.
Friends and family don't believe in my dreams.
I have faith I can make it and my heart screams.
Where do I go from here?
I'm moving on.
I failed my test.
I did my best.
Where do I go from here?
I'm moving on.
Dating isn't working for me.
I decided I want to be free.
Where do I go from here?
I'm moving on.
Whenever life pitches me a curve ball.
Winter, spring, summer, or fall.
I swing because I can answer that call.
Where do I go from here?
I'm moving on.

Out of the park.
All I needed was a spark.
I will never remain in the dark.
Where do i go from here?
I'll always keep moving on!

Blossom

25

Pigtails and hair bows with ribbons of all sorts.
Overalls and plaid shirts, or t-shirts with cute
skirts and shorts.
Rock n Rolls, tennis shoes, and cowgirl boots.
Fresh silk pressed or curly hair.
Tank tops and leggings or Sunday dresses with
a cancan flare.
Shiny dress shoes and colorful sandals worn
with care.
Cornrows, braids, and fancy bobs adorned as a
goddess.
Dressy shirts, Jazzy jeans and sundresses.
High heels on fleek and high tops stylish for
fun.
Classy curls hanging down the back or pinned
up in a fancy bun.
A-line sassy dresses and colorful business attire.
Glittery and Classy high heels and flats full of
fire.
Always dressed for success when she's seen.
A princess blossomed into a queen.

Maternity

A new life grows within me.
It's a miracle for all to see.
God has given me a great responsibility.
A childhood dream is now my reality.
I never knew how concerned I would be.
Praying more now, constantly seeking thee.
I am cautious.
Feeling more nauseous.
Conscious of everything I eat and drink.
Definitely avoiding anything with a stink.
I sleep most of the day.
I even cry when things don't go my way.
Walking around with a glow.
So many things I don't know.
Doctor visits are a must.
So is having one I trust.
My baby is growing bigger.
Moving around like Tigger.
My love for my baby is great.
Other mothers can relate.
Doing everything for my baby's survival.
I am anxious for my baby's arrival.

From Within My Heart

From within my heart,
I love others as I love myself.
From within my heart,
I place all hate on a shelf.
From within my heart,
I care.
From within my heart,
I share.
From within my heart,
I show compassion.
From within my heart,
I take action.
From within my heart,
I sing with soul.
From within my heart,
I remain whole.
From within my heart,
I share God's word.
From within my heart,
I pray my voice is heard.
From within my heart,
I know God is in control.
From within my heart,
I keep my joy from being stole.
From within my heart,

I shall forever give God praise.
From within my heart,
I shall keep my hands raised.
From within my heart,
I will trust the Lord all my days.